Y0-DJQ-409

NGARI, TIBET

西藏阿里

FOREIGN LANGUAGES PRESS　BEIJING

外文出版社　北京

NGARI, TIBET

Ngari(It has different ways of transliteration ,such as mNgav-ris and Ali, etc.), a miraculous district in the west of the Tibet Autonomous Region in China, is called "the ridge on the Roof of the World". The Himalaya Mountain, the Kunlun Mountain and the *Kailas* (Gangsri-ti-se) Mountain surround it. Ngari, with a meaning of "an area under one's jurisdiction" in Tibetan language, is also called "the third extreme of life" because of its average altitude of 4,500 meters above sea level (Some places are above the snowline.) The Elephant River (gLang-chen kha-vbabs, a river from the mouth of the elephant-shaped rock), the Horse River (rTa-mchog kha-vbabs, a river from the mouth of the horse-shaped rock), the Peacock River (rMa-bya kha-vbabs, a river from the mouth of the peacock-shaped rock) and the Lion River (Seng-ge kha-vbabs, a river from the mouth of the lion-shaped rock) flow from the *Kailas* Mountain. They form respectively four rivers at the maximum altitude above sea level in the world. The Horse River, the upper reaches of the Yar-klung-gtsang-po River, is named "the Heavenly River"and the other three rivers, which are regarded as"Holy Waters" flow through Nepal, Kashmir Region, India and Bangladesh and then pour into the Indian Ocean.

Ngari Region is 600 kilometers long from the east to the west and 550 kilometers wide from the south to the north. Seven counties are under its jurisdiction, such as dGe-rgyas

County, sPu-hreng County, Ru-thog County and others. Ngari Region occupies an area of 312,796 square kilometers and has a population of only 62,500 people, which is an administrative region with the largest geographical area in China now and the lowest population density in the world. Ngari is more than 1,800 kilometers apart from Lhasa, capital of Tibet. It lies in the remote area, but in Tibet and among other Tibetan-inhabited areas, such as Qinghai, Gansu, Yunnan and Sichuan, it is one of the most influential and popular tourist sites at home and abroad.

From the mid-9th century to the first half of the 17th century, there once existed the Gu-ge Kingdom, which was in fashion for a time and had a population of over 100,000 people. Nowadays, through all hardships, the kingdom with the glory of a thousand years has turned into dilapidated halls and walls reaching to the sky. Only desolation and misery was left, but it still remains its imposing manner and ancient customs, becoming one of the sacred sites of great historical value on the Tibetan Plateau. Bon was a primitive religion before the introduction of Buddhism into Tibet. It originated from Ngari and was spread into Tibetan hinterland and other Tibetan-inhabited areas from there. There are large numbers of monasteries and temples, such as mTho-gling Monastery, vKhor-chags Monastery and several tens of historical sites and ruins in Ngari. With a history of over a thousand years, they have not only exerted important influence on the development of Tibetan Buddhism, but also are of great value for the understanding of the history of Ngari Region and politics, economics, cultures and religions of the whole Tibetan Plateau. Thousand-Buddha Cave in rTsa-mdav County is in the same historical position as the Gu-ge Kingdom. Dong-dkar and Phyi-dbang frescoes in the Thousand-Buddha Cave still remain undeveloped, which are important cultural relics to be further verified. Rock paintings in dozens of sites within the territory of Ru-thog County in the northern Ngari are absolutely rated superb masterpieces. They have distinctly recorded productive contents and the way of life of their ancestors in Ngari. Thus it can be seen that the history of Ngari has undoubtedly constituted the most important component in the history of the development of Tibet.

Everything in Ngari is related to religions. From the time immemorial, hundreds of millions of believers of Bonism, Buddhism, Hinduism and Jaina respectfully regard Ngari as "the core of the universe" where holy spirits inhabit. They have a common worship to Gangs-rin-po-che, the Holy Mountain and Ma-pham-g· yu-mtsho, the Holy Lake with a water area of 412 square kilometers. Every year, they attract tens of thousands of tourists and pilgrims from India, Nepal, Japan, Europe and America and believers from Tibetan-inhabited areas, such as Tibet, Qinghai, Gansu, Yunnan and Sichuan to go for a circumambulation around the Holy Mountain and the Holy Lake to pay their homage to them.

The scene in Ngari is both miraculous and charming. Blue ripples are on sPang-gong-mtsho Bird Island, which is rarely seen in plateau topography. Ten thousands of gulls are perching there. The northwest of Ngari is the world well-known Depopulated Zone of the Northern Tibet. It lies between 5,000 and 6,000 meters above sea level. Its area is vast and its air is very thin. The depopulated zone is wild and uninhabited, but it is a natural paradise for numerous wild animals. There live several ten kinds of world's rare wild animals, such as Tibetan wild asses, Tibetan yaks, Tibetan antelopes, black-necked cranes and snow leopards. Ngari Plateau is one of the best regions where national ecology and wild animals are well preserved due to its maximum altitude above sea level and its inconvenient transportation.

On China's territory, Ngari is an area with the maximum altitude above sea level, the bluest sky, the most mysterious historical sites, the lowest population density and the well-preserved wild animals. If you go to Tibet, but not to visit Ngari, you will have a lifelong regret. Ngari reveals a grand historic scene, which is not only a land of reality where spirits and beliefs root, but also a holy land on Tibetan Plateau for people to purify their souls.

西藏阿里

在中国西藏自治区西部，有一片神奇的地域，那就是被世人称为"世界屋脊之屋脊"的阿里地区。阿里，藏语意为"辖区"，为喜马拉雅山山脉、昆仑山脉和冈底斯山脉诸峰所环抱，因其平均海拔4500米，有些地方甚至高于雪线，所以这里又被称为"生命第三极"。冈底斯山脉四周溢出的象泉河、马泉河、孔雀河和狮泉河分别形成了全球海拔最高的四大河流，而马泉河即雅鲁藏布江的上游，被称为"天河"，其他三条河流分别通过尼泊尔、克什米尔地区、印度和孟加拉注入印度洋，被称为"圣水"。

阿里地区东西长600公里、南北宽500公里，辖措勤、革吉、普兰和日土等七县，面积312,796平方公里，全地区人口仅6.25万人，是中国目前地理面积最大的地区行政区，也是世界上人口密度最小的地区。阿里距西藏首府拉萨尚有1800余公里，虽地处偏僻，然而，在西藏全地区乃至青海、甘肃、云南和四川其他所有藏区中，阿里却一直是国内外最富影响、最热门的旅游地区之一。

公元9世纪中叶至17世纪上半叶，这里曾出现过盛极一时、人口逾十万的古格王国。如今，在饱经历史磨难之后，这段千年前的辉煌早已化为残殿断壁耸立于天际，留下的只有苍凉与神秘、气势不减、古风犹存，成为雪域高原最有历史价值的圣地之一。本教是佛教传入西藏前的一种原始宗教，它发源于阿里，也是从这里传入西藏腹地和其他藏区的。阿里地区留存着已有千年历史、对西藏佛教发展产生过重要影响的托林寺和科迦寺等众多寺庙和数十处历史古迹、遗址，它们对于了解阿里地区的历史和整个西藏高原的政治、经济、文化、宗教都极具价值；位于札达县、与古格王国遗址历史地位相当的千年佛窟中的东嘎、皮旺壁画，是尚未开发、有待进一步考证的另一处重要文化遗址；阿里地区北部日土县境内的数十处岩画更是堪称一绝，它清晰地记录了阿里先民们的生产内容和生活方式。由此可见，阿里的历史无疑构成了整个西藏地区发展史中最重要的组成部分。

阿里的一切都离不开宗教，从远古起，本教、佛教、印度教、耆那教等多种宗教的亿万信徒就将阿里尊为圣灵之所在的"世界中心"，他们共同崇拜的神山冈仁布钦和拥有412平方公里水域的圣湖玛旁雍措，每年都吸引着成千上万来自印度、尼泊尔、日本和欧美等国的旅游者、香客以及西藏、青海、甘肃、云南和四川藏区的信教群众前来转山、转湖、朝拜。

阿里的雪域风光神奇而迷人，高原地形中极其少见的鸟岛——班公湖鸟岛，碧波荡漾，栖息着数以万计的鸥鸟；阿里的西北部，就是闻名于世的藏北无人区，海拔在5000－6000米之间，地域广阔，空气稀薄。无人区虽寥无人烟，却是众多野生动物的天然乐园，生活着藏野驴、藏牦牛、藏羚羊、黑颈鹤、雪豹等数十种世界珍稀野生动物。由于海拔高，交通不便，因此阿里高原又是自然生态与野生动物保护最好的区域之一。

在中国的版图上，阿里的海拔最高，天最蓝，历史古迹最富神秘性，人烟最稀少，而野生动物生态又保存得最完好。到了西藏，若不踏足阿里，将会使人留下终生的遗憾。阿里夹裹着一幕宏大的历史风景，它是精神与信仰落脚的一片现实的土地，不愧为净化人心灵的雪域圣地。

Puddles on Ngari Wasteland

"Haizi" means naturally accumulated puddles. The larger ones have the same size as lakes while the smaller ones just look like puddles."Haizi"has become a wonder on Ngari Plateau because of drought and rare rains.

阿里荒原 "海子"

"海子"、天然积水坑、大如湖、小如坑。由于阿里高原严重干旱少雨、故 "海子" 就成为高原一大奇景。

8

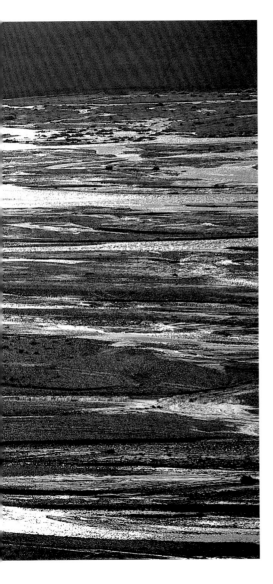

The Dawn on the Elephant River

Ngari Plateau is called "the Summit of Thousands of Mountains and the Source of Ten Thousands of Waters". The Lion River, the Elephant River, the Peacock River and the Horse River named after four animals in the Kingdom of Heaven all originate from the *Kailas* Mountain. They respectively become the sources of the famous Indus, Ganges in South Asia and Yar-klung-gtsang-po River. This is the Elephant River flowing through the territory of rTsa-mdav County.

象泉河之晨

阿里高原号称"千山之巅、万水之源"，以天国之中的马、狮、象、孔雀四种动物命名的狮泉河、象泉河、孔雀河、马泉河均源于冈底斯山，而它们又分别成为南亚著名的印度河、恒河和雅鲁藏布江之源。这是流经札达县境内的象泉河。

10

Mani Stone Piles

Tibetan people are a nationality whose
people all believe in religions. Religions penetrate every levels of social
life. People place stone piles or stone
plates engraved with Buddha's words,
images of Buddha and Six Sacred Words
on roadsides, mountain passes, holy
mountains and lake banks or in monasteries or in front of images of Buddha,
showing their blessings and pray.

玛尼石堆

藏族是一个全民信教的民族，宗教渗透于
社会生活的各个层面。人们在路边、山口
以及寺庙、神山、圣湖、佛像等处堆放上
刻有佛语、佛像、六字真言的石块、石板
等，以示祝福、祈祷。

11

rTsa-mdav Earth Forest

rTsa-mdav Earth Forest, called "horizontal bedded landforms" in geomorphology, came to peculiar "secondary tectonic landforms" through erosion by flowing water. They are sedimentary beds of lakes and rivers in the Pliocene Epoch, mainly consisting of fine sand rocks and clay mixed with coarse gravel rocks. Deep valleys and chilly gorges constitute majestic tall and straight ancient walls and castles in varied shapes and styles. Such miraculous and magnificent earth forests encircle according to the lie of the mountains and are scattered in several hundred kilometers in rTsa-mdav County.

札达土林

在地貌学上称"水平岩层地貌"，是经过流水侵蚀形成的比较特殊的次生构造地貌，为上新世湖泊和河流的沉积地层，以粉细砂岩和粘土为主、间夹粗砂砾岩。沟谷深邃、谷坡陡立、形成雄伟挺拔、奇异多姿的古城墙和古城堡形态。如此神奇壮观的土林地貌、依山势环绕、密布于札达县数百平方公里范围内。

The Gu-ge Kingdom

From the ninth to the seventeenth century, descendents of the Tu-bo Dynasty separated Tibetan local regime. And in the Gu-ge Kingdom, there were altogether 16 kings who succeeded to the throne. This photo shows the central part of the Gu-ge Kingdom. In the mid-seventeenth century, the Ladakh invaded the Gu-ge Kingdom and destroyed it. Among extant ruins, the Red Temple, the White Temple, *Mandala*, the Palace Hall and the Palace of *Dharmapala* (Protector of *Dharma*) are most magnificent. Frescoes, sculptures and stone engravings of different styles in the Gu-ge Ruins are the most precious and of great historical and artistic value.

古格王国

公元9－17世纪，吐蕃王朝后裔在西藏的地方割据政权。古格王朝世袭了16代国王，图为古格王国的中心。公元17世纪中叶，王国被外来的拉达克人入侵毁坏。现存遗址中以红庙、白庙、坛城、王宫殿、护法神殿最为壮观。古格遗址中风格各异的壁画、雕塑和石刻更为珍贵，具有极高的史料和艺术价值。

The Gu-ge Ruins

The Gu-ge Ruins lies on a 30-meter-high mound, 18 kilometers apart from the Lion River County. The main body of the ruins occupies an area of 180,000 square meters. It has been verified that there are 445 house ruins, 879 caves, 58 watchtowers, hundreds of *stupas* of all kinds and 10 successive defensive walls in the ruins. A weaponry, a cave burial site, a wall burial site and an earth burial site have been found already. The Royal Palace stood on the top of the cliff. Most of monks' premises were built on halfway up the mountain while houses owned by common people centered at the foot of the mountain.

古格遗迹

位于距狮泉河镇18公里的一座高约300米的土岗上。遗址主体总面积约18万平方米。已查实房屋遗址445座、洞窟879孔、碉楼58座、各类佛塔上百座、防卫墙10道;发现武器库1座、洞葬、壁葬、土葬各一处。王宫居于山崖之顶,寺院僧舍大部分建在山腰、老百姓的民居集中于山脚。

Gu-ge Red Palace

It is also called "Red Temple"(Lha-khang-dmar-po in Tibetan Language) for its red color painted on the palace walls. The Red Palace, facing the east, occupies an area of 300 square meters, whose gates are decorated with relief decorations and Six Sanskrit Words are engraved in the central part of both gates. The relief figures on the frames of both gates are vivid and elegant. There are 36 pillars within the temple and flowers, plants and animals in different vivid modeling are colorfully painted on its ceilings.

古格红宫

又称红庙、藏语为"拉康玛波"，因宫墙上涂红而得名、面积300平方米。它坐西朝东、大门浮雕纹饰、中间刻有六字真言、门框浮雕人物形象生动典雅、庙内有36根柱子、天花板上彩绘各种造型生动的花卉和动物。

18

Gu-ge Ruins, Incense Burners and Streamers

They embody the feelings of reverence and worship that people have today for deities in Gu-ge.

19

古格的废墟、香炉与经幢

这是今人对古格神灵的敬畏与崇拜。

Gu-ge Cave

Its outer walls have been eroded by wind, but its interior still remains solemn colors, telling the glorious history of the past.

古格洞窟

外壁早已被风蚀、内窟却依然保留着述说当年辉煌历史的凝重色彩。

Gu-ge Statues of Buddha

Sculptures of various kinds in Gu-ge Ruins have a distinctive style. All the human figures are lifelike. Male statues are very strong and take on a handsome look while female ones have full and round breasts, large buttocks and slender and graceful waists. Generally, the statue has a slender figure and is sculptured in an exaggerated way. This is one of the characteristics which differs from the sculptural art in other places of Tibet.

古格佛像

古格遗址中的各种雕塑别具一格，人物形象更是栩栩如生。男性塑像体魄强健、面貌英俊，女性塑像隆乳丰臀、腰肢婀娜。一般塑像身体修长，雕塑手法夸张，这是与西藏其他地方的塑像艺术有所不同的特点之一。

Decorations on the Top of the Hall

Tops of halls in Gu-gē are peculiar in modeling and bright and beautiful in color. There are nearly 500 kinds of patterns only on the ceilings. Some are rhombus. Some are painted with different kinds of flower, plant and animal designs. The compositions are free and charming and full of rich imagination.

殿顶装饰

古格各佛殿顶部造型奇特、色彩艳丽、仅天花板图案就有约500种、有的为菱形、有的绘满了各种花卉、动物图案、构图自由、想象丰富、极具魅力。

23

Gu-ge Frescoes

The frescoes are much more colorful and varied in Gu-ge than in other areas of Tibet. Apart from common Buddhas, *Bodhisattvas*, Mother of All Deities (Yumchen), Heavenly Kings, Protectors of *Vajra*, eminent monks, the virtues and Buddhist stories, there are some peculiar frescoes, showing that fresco art in Gu-ge was not only influenced by alien arts, but also formed its own peculiar artistic style. They were a thousand years ago.

古格壁画

远比西藏其他地区的壁画丰富多彩。除反映常见的佛、菩萨、佛母、天王、护法金刚、高僧大德及佛教故事等等之外，还有许多独特的壁画形象。显示出古格壁画艺术既受到外来艺术的诸多影响，又自成风格。这些壁画距今已有千年的历史。

24

Gu-ge Cave Frescoes

On the left side is a picture of sacrificial rites. The scene on this fresco was played up exciting and was dense in color and luster. On the right side is a picture of Mother of All Deities (Yumchen). The lines on it are very fluent. She takes on an elegant appearance, kind and reserved.

古格洞穴壁画

左为祭祀庆典图、场面被渲染得激动人心、装饰色块浓重。右为佛母图、硬笔线条流畅、佛母形象高雅、慈祥而内隐。

Shields, Helmets, Armors and Arrow Shafts Excavated in Gu-ge Ruins

Shields, round in shape, are made of rattans and wrapped with leather stripes. There is a conical iron top in the central part. They are exquisitely made and very sturdy. According to textual research, it is one of military equipments during the Tu-bo period.

古格遗址中出土的盾牌、盔甲、箭杆等物

盾牌呈圆形，用藤条编制，后用皮条加捆，中间还有一圆锥铁顶，制作精致而坚固。据考证，这是吐蕃时期军队的装备之一。

27

Gu-ge 108 *Stupas* Forest

According to Buddhist theory, *stupas* have eight styles, symbolizing the eight virtuous deeds made by Sakyamuni in his whole life. The number of *stupas* is based on Buddhist scriptures. "*Stupa*", representing ideals, truth and masters' advice, is the Body of *Dharma*. Building stupas means practicing Buddhism.

古格一百零八座佛塔林

佛教理论上所讲的塔的八种类型、象征释迦牟尼一生的八种功德。108座塔的取数即依照佛经要求而来。"塔"代表了理想、真谛及大师的训诫、就是法身、修佛塔即修佛身。

Dong-dkar Buddha Grotto

The word of "Dong-dkar" in Tibetan has a meaning of "white conch". It lies in a narrow area on halfway up the mountain in rTsa-mdav County 40 kilometers apart from the Gu-ge Kingdom. Dong-dkar Cave is the earliest aged and well-preserved Buddhist art remains in Ngari, where frescoes, plentiful in content, are Tibetan Buddhist art treasures.

东嘎佛窟

东嘎藏语意为"白海螺"，位于札达县距古格王国遗址40公里处一处狭长地带的山腰上。东嘎佛窟是目前阿里地区发现年代最早、保存较完好、壁画内容极为丰富的佛教艺术遗存，其壁画是藏传佛教艺术珍品。

Dong-dkar Frescoes have a well-knit composition, fluent lines and splendid colors, whose modeling is very peculiar and lifelike. The frescoes are rich in content and have a long history. The themes center on Buddhist stories. On frescoes are painted images of Buddhas, Protectors of Dharma, Guardians and pictures depicting Buddha's preaching and decorative patterns of all kinds, such as peacocks, dragon-fish, a pair of intertwined dragons and a pair of phoenixes standing opposite each other and Mandalas of Tantric Buddhism. Most of designs on the frescoes are fairy (asparas), who have a vivid modeling and varied styles. There are also many engravings and pictures depicting alien figures. The frescoes were painted in special natural mineral colors, which still remain new through ages and never fade.

东嘎壁画构图严谨、线条流畅、色彩鲜艳、造型独特、栩栩如生。壁画内容丰富、历史久远，题材主要围绕佛教故事，有佛像、护法神、力士像、说法图，还有孔雀、龙鱼及双龙缠绕、双凤对立等各种装饰图案纹样及密宗曼陀罗等。壁画中天女图案最多，造型生动、变化丰富，也有许多异国他乡的人物刻画。壁画采用特殊的天然矿物颜料绘制，经久犹新、几不褪色。

Dong-dkar Frescoes

东嘎壁画

Dong-dkar Frescoes
东嘎壁画

33

Dong-dkar Frescoes
东嘎壁画

Gangs-rin-po-che — the Holy Mountain

Gangs-rin-po-che, the main summit of the *Kailas* Mountain, lies at the altitude of 6,714 meters above sea level. Gangs-rin-po-che means "Treasure of the Snow Mountain" in Tibetan language, which is the Holy Mountain worshipped by believers of Bonism, Buddhism, Jaina and Hinduism. Tradition has it that Guardians of Deities, *Bodhisattvas*, heavenly gods, *Ausras* (demons of the higher order) and musicians in the Realm of Heaven gathered around the Holy Mountain while *Sakyamuni* was still alive on earth. That year happened to be the Horse Year. Therefore, the Horse Year became Gangs-rin-po-che's destined year. According to the legend, a pilgrim can redress all the sins committed in his whole life by going on a circulumation around the Holy Mountain. If ten circles, he can avoid going into hell within the five hundred circles of existence (*Samsara*). If one hundred circles, he can become a Buddha and enter the Realm of Heaven. If one circle in the Horse Year, an extra circle with twelve merits will be added, which is equal to thirteen circles in an ordinary year. The temptation from the Holy Mountain and reverence showed by people for thousands of years makes pilgrims in an endless stream go on a circulumation every year.

神山冈仁布钦

冈底斯山的主峰，海拔6714米，藏语意为"雪山之宝"。它是本教、佛教、耆那教、印度教等
多种宗教共奉的神山。相传佛祖释迦牟尼尚在人间时，守护之神、诸菩萨、天神、阿修罗和天
界乐师等都云集在神山周围，时值马年，因此马年便成为冈仁布钦的本命年。相传朝圣者来绕
山转一圈，可洗净一生罪孽；转十圈可在五百轮回中免下地狱之苦；转百圈可在今生成佛升天；
而在马年转一圈，则可增加一轮十二功德，相当于常年的十三圈。千百年来神山的诱惑和众人
的崇拜，使转山朝圣者年复一年、络绎不绝。

38

Driving Yaks to Go on a Circulumation around the Holy Mountain

As the road of paying homage to the Holy Mountain is full of hardships, many foreign pilgrims have to set out half a year earlier.

赶牦牛转山

朝圣之道神圣而艰辛，许多国外香客甚至须提前半年启程。

An Indian Pilgrim
印度香客

People Going on a Circulumation around the Holy Mountain

转山人

41

Mani Stone Piles and Banners and Streamers on the Road to the Holy Mountain

转山路上的玛尼石堆和经幡。

Ruins Complex of mTho-gling Monastery

Built in the second half of the tenth century, mTho-gling Monastery was originally named "mTho-lding Monastery", which means "Hovering Monastery". This monastery, modeled after a Buddhist monastery in Ancient India, became the source of the Upper Route of Expounding Buddhism in the Later Prosperity of Tibetan Buddhism, which played a decisive role in Tibetan history. In the period of great prosperity, it possessed 25 subordinate monasteries within the territory of the Three Regions of Nagri. The whole complex consisted of Sa-kya Hall, the White Hall, the Hall of Eighteen *Arhats*, the Hall of *Maitreya*, the Hall of Protectors of *Dharma*, the Assembly Hall and numerous Mani Houses, monks' premises Bla-brang (high-ranking lamas' residence) and 108 stupas. It is a magnificent building complete, narrow in the south and north and wide in the east and the west.

托林寺群落遗址

托林寺建于公元 10 世纪后半叶,原名"托丁寺",意为飞翔之寺,仿古印度佛教寺院形制建造,为藏传佛教后弘期上路弘法之策源地,在藏族历史上有举足轻重的地位。在鼎盛时期,它拥有遍布阿里三围的 25 座属寺。整个群落由萨迦殿、白殿、十八罗汉殿、弥勒佛殿、护法神殿、集合殿以及众多的玛尼房、僧舍、喇让以及 108 座佛塔构成,南北窄、东西宽,是一处宏伟的建筑群。

mTho-gling Monastery Ruins

A 10-meter-high pagoda in the ruins, simple and elegant, is the notable symbol of mTho-gling Monastery. Far behind it, stands a magnificent Decency Pagoda.

托林寺遗迹

废墟中10余米高的塔身、形色雅拙、成为托林寺的显著标志。背后远处是颇具气势的风化塔。

46

Frescoes in mTho-gling Monastery

The frescoes in mTho-gling Monastery are colorful, magnificent and elegant and the figures on them are of natural grace.

托林寺壁画

形色华丽古雅，情致飘逸。

Sculptures in mTho-
gling Monastery

托林寺塑像

47

48

bsTan-vdzin-dbang-grags, Bonpo Living Buddha (Rin-po-che)

He is an abbot of the only Bonpo monastery surviving in Ngari Region.

本教活佛丹增旺扎

他是阿里地区唯存的一座本教寺院的住持。

49

gShung-po Monastery

This monastery, built in the early seventeenth century, used to be the largest one among the four main monasteries in Ngari Region. In the past, it was used as the winter residence for the local government of sPu-hreng rDzong. It used to possess 250 rooms. Whenever the monastery celebrated its festivals, all the gates would be opened. Lamas would chant Buddhist scriptures together, forming a grand scene. Nowadays, it remains its original state.

雄波寺

建于17世纪初，曾是阿里地区四大寺庙中最庞大者，旧时是普兰宗政府的冬日驻地。原有房屋250间，逢寺院节日、庙门具开、喇嘛集体念经、场面宏大。如今这里的一切都归于原色。

Frescoes in vKhor-chags Monastery

vKhor-chags Monastery, built in 1088, 20 kilometers
apart from sPu-hreng, is of a cordial and secular sense
due to its compact layout together with monks' premises
and ordinary houses.

科迦寺壁画

科迦寺建于1088年、距普兰20公里、因与僧舍、民房坐落
紧凑、而具有一种亲近和世俗的意味。

Religious Activities
佛事活动

dGon-pa Monastery

Built on halfway up the mountain in sPu-hreng County, it can only be reached through an aerial plank road built along the face of a cliff. The temple consisted of numerous caves where large numbers of frescoes and Buddhist texts were kept. Tradition has it that it was the Winter Palace owned by Prince Nor-bzang, who was the figure in *Prince Nor-bzang*, one of the eight Tibetan operas.

贡巴寺

建于普兰县一个半山腰上，须经悬空栈道才能进入。寺庙由数间山洞组成，内有许多壁画和经书。相传这是西藏八大藏戏之一《诺桑王子》中诺桑王子的冬宫。

rTsa-mdav-spu-hreng Monastery

It is the access that people must follow to pay homage to Gangs-rin-po-che, the Holy Mountain. It is also the key to open the gates to going on a circulumation. Without it, people can not go into the mountain. According to the legend, this is the Practice Palace owned by *Atisa*, Ancient Indian scholar and eminent Buddhist monk. In 1042, at the invitation of Ye-shes-vod, the king of the Gu-ge Kingdom, he entered Tibet, preaching Buddhist texts and medicine, translating Buddhist scriptures and teaching disciples. He exerted great influence on the spread and development of Tibetan Buddhism. Tradition has it that there exists a large rock with *Atisa*'s footprints on it in rTsa-mdav-spu-hreng Monastery.

札达普兰寺

这是朝圣神山冈仁布钦必去的地方。它是转山开门的钥匙、不拿钥匙无法进山。据说这里是古印度学者、佛教高僧阿底峡的修行宫。1042 年他受古格王益西沃之邀、进藏传播佛法和医学、译经授徒、对西藏佛教的传播发展产生了很大影响。传说札达普兰寺内依然留存着有阿底峡足印的大石头。

A Elderly Monk
老僧人

56

Ma-pham-g˙yu-mtsho, the Holy Lake

This Holy Lake, at the altitude of 4,582 meters above sea level, is regarded as
"the Mother of Rivers". She is the wife of the "Holy Mountain" in legends.

圣湖玛旁雍措
海拔 4582 米，被视为 "江河之母"，神话传说是 "神山" 的妻子。

gNas-mo-sna-gnyis Peak at the Altitude of 7,728 Meters above Sea Level and La-lnga-mtsho, the Ghost Lake. The surface of the lake is always covered with clouds and mists, spreading a moist and surreptitious atmosphere.

海拔7728米的纳木那尼峰与鬼湖拉昂措。湖面常被云雾所笼罩、迷漫着一层潮湿而诡秘的气氛。

Ru-thog rDzong Ruins

The word of "Ru-thog" in Tibetan language has a meaning of "on the mountain" while the word of "rDzong" means "old government". So Ru-thog rDzong represents Tibetan local government set up on the mountaintop. In the former site of Ru-thog rDzong, there still stands Ru-thog Monastery. Built in about 1337, Ru-thog Monastery is also called "Lhun-grub-chos-ldan". Plenty of Buddhist scriptures and other cultural relics are preserved there.

日土宗遗址

"日土"藏语意为山上、"宗"即旧政府，全意就是昔日建在山顶上的西藏地方政权。在日土宗旧址上，至今还保存着日土寺。日土寺又称"伦珠曲登"，约建于1337年，寺内保留有不少经书和其他文物。

60

Ru-thog Rock Paintings

Ancestors in Ngari engraved these rock paintings on the mountain rocks. It can be seen from the patterns and designs that the natural environment was quite fit for people to live.

日土岩画

阿里先民勾凿于山岩上，由其图案可见昔时当地的自然环境还相当适宜人们居住。

Black-necked Cranes
黑颈鹤

63

sPang-gong-mtsho Bird Island
班公湖鸟岛

64

Ngari Pasture
阿里牧场

Wild Asses in Natural Preservation Zone
自然保护区内的野驴

The Lion River Town at the Altitude
of 4,300 Meters above Sea Level

狮泉河镇，海拔 4300 米。

The Elephant River

It is called "gLang-chen-bzang-po" in Tibetan language, which flows
towards India from the east to the west. In the past, it irrigated over
one hundred thousand pieces of oases. Now it is encircled by layers of
earth forests and vast and bare Gobi Desert.

象泉河

藏语称"朗钦藏布"，由东向西流往印度，当年它灌溉着养育十万余众的绿
洲，如今却为层层土林和广袤的戈壁荒漠所包围。

68

Tibetans Living in the Depths of the Plateau
生活在高原深处的藏民

Mobile Family
流动人家

Xinjiang–Tibet Road
新藏公路

新疆维吾尔自治区 Xinjiang Uygur Autonomous Region

班公湖
Bangong Co Lake

鸟岛
Bird Island

日土
Rutog

藏北野生动物乐园
Paradise for wild Lives in Northern Tibet

噶尔 狮泉河
Ge'er
Shiquan River

狮泉河镇
Shiquanhe Township

朗久地热
Geothermal
energy at Langjiu

革吉
Gegyai

底雅
Tiya

古格王朝遗址
Ruins of Guge Kingdom

扎达
Zanda

土林 Forest of Earth

象泉河
Xiangquan River

Gangdise

拉昂措
Lha-ang
Co Lake

冈仁布钦 (神山)
Mt. Kanqrinboqe (Holy Mountain)

玛旁雍措 (圣湖)
Mapam Yumco (Sacred Lake)

纳木那尼峰
Mt Neimona'nyi ▲

普兰
Burang

科迦寺
Korchag Temple

那曲地区 Naqu Prefecture

措勤
Coqen

扎日南木措
Zhari Namco Lake

印度
INDIA

尼泊尔
NEPAL

Himalayas

西藏阿里旅游略图
TOURIST MAP OF NGARI, TIBET

日喀则地区
Xigaze Prefecture

图书在版编目（CIP）数据

西藏阿里：英汉／成卫东编。—北京：外文出版社，1999.2
ISBN 7-119-02344-6

Ⅰ．西… Ⅱ．成… Ⅲ．风光摄影－西藏－阿里地区－摄影集 Ⅳ．J426.752
中国版本图书馆 CIP 数据核字（98）第 38520 号

Compiled and Text by: Cheng Weidong
Photos by: Cheng Weidong
Translated by: Xiang Hongjia
Edited by: Wei Aijun
Designed by: Yuan Qing

编撰：成卫东
摄影：成卫东
翻译：向红笳
责任编辑：韦爱君
设计：元　青

西藏阿里

成卫东　编

First Edition 1999

Ngari, Tibet

ISBN 7-119-02344-6

© Foreign Languages Press
Published by Foreign Languages Press
24 Baiwanzhuang Road, Beijing 100037, China
Home Page: http://www.flp.com.cn
E-mail Addresses: info @ flp.com.cn
　　　　　　　　 sales @ flp.com.cn
Printed in the People's Republic of China

© 外文出版社
外文出版社出版
（中国北京百万庄大街 24 号）
邮政编码 100037
外文出版社网页：http://www.flp.com.cn
外文出版社电子邮件地址：info @ flp.com.cn
　　　　　　　　　　　　 sales @ flp.com.cn
天时印刷（深圳）有限公司印刷
1999 年（24 开）第一版
1999 年第一版第一次印刷
（英汉）
ISBN 7-119-02344-6/J · 1473（外）
004800（精）